THE Tigger MOVIE

Ladybird

It was autumn, and Tigger was bouncing through the Hundred Acre Wood. Tigger loved bouncing. But he wanted someone to bounce with him, so he bounced over to Pooh's house.

"Hi, Pooh Boy!" he cried. "Wanna go bouncin'?"

"Oh, I can't," Pooh replied. "I need to collect enough honey pots for the winter."

So Tigger bounced on...

Soon Tigger met up with Piglet. Then he bounced past Kanga. But all Tigger's friends were too busy to go bouncing with him. Everyone was getting ready for winter. But there was another reason why they didn't want to go bouncing…

"The problem is," said Piglet, when the friends were all together later that day, "we can't bounce like Tiggers because…"

"Well… because we're *not* Tiggers," said Pooh, sadly.

Poor Tigger wandered off into the woods. He suddenly felt very lonely. But just when he was feeling his droopiest, Roo appeared.

"Tigger," Roo said, "maybe you aren't alone. Maybe you have a family somewhere."

"A family fulla Tiggers! Can you imagine such a thing?" Tigger cried excitedly. "We could all bounce the Whoop-de-Dooper Bounce!"

So the two friends went to Owl's house to ask him how to find Tigger's family.

"You need to find your family tree," Owl explained.

"A family tree!" cried Tigger. "Let's go, Roo Boy!"

Tigger and Roo went to the woods to begin their search. But they couldn't find Tigger's family tree anywhere. At last, Tigger decided to return home. He was very upset.

As Roo bounced into Tigger's house, he had an idea.

"Why don't you write your family a letter?" he suggested.

And that's exactly what Tigger did. He dropped the letter into the postbox and waited for a reply.

Meanwhile, Pooh, Piglet and Eeyore had decided to look for Tigger's family, too. They found some stripey, bouncing creatures by the pond, but they didn't seem quite right!

Poor Tigger waited… and waited… and waited. As the snow began to fall Roo had to go home. He felt bad about leaving Tigger alone when he was so unhappy. So the next day, Roo called everyone together.

"Let's pretend to be Tigger's family and write him a letter to cheer him up," he said.

The friends wrote a fine letter – one they knew that Tigger would like.

Sure enough, the next day Tigger woke his friends and showed them the letter from his family. He was very excited.

Tigger's friends were pleased to see him so happy. But then he said, "And they're all coming to visit tomorrow!"

Nobody remembered putting that in the letter!

Roo wanted to tell Tigger the truth, but Tigger was so happy that Roo didn't want to upset him.

The friends didn't know what to do. Finally, Roo had another idea.

"Let's pretend to be Tigger's family. We'll act real tiggery and dress up."

And so that's what the friends decided to do.

"Ya finally made it!" Tigger cried when he saw them approaching his house. "Let's bounce!"

The friends bounced around and Roo tried the Whoop-de-Dooper Bounce. But suddenly Roo tripped and lost his mask. Tigger was heartbroken. He thought his friends were playing a joke on him.

"There's a *real* Tigger family out there, and I'm gonna find them," he said. "T-T-F-E – Ta-Ta-For-Ever!" he cried and headed for the door.

Roo was miserable. The next day he went to see Pooh in tears. He wanted Tigger to come home, and so the friends all went out in the snow to find him.

In another part of the wood, Tigger had found a huge tree.

"That's it!" he cried. "My family tree! Tigger family, are ya there?"

But Tigger got no reply. All alone in the snow, Tigger climbed up into the tree.

But Tigger wasn't really alone. His friends had found him and were close by.

Suddenly, there was a rumbling noise. As Tigger jumped down from the tree he saw a huge pile of snow racing towards his friends!

Tigger quickly bounced everyone to safety, but he got swept away in the snow. Determined to save his friend, Roo bounced a Whoop-de-Dooper and rescued Tigger.

"You saved my life, Roo Boy!" Tigger exclaimed.

It didn't take Tigger long to realise that his real family had been there with him all along.

When they got home, Tigger had a big party for his friends and he gave them all presents. He even gave Roo his family locket. Once again, the friends were together as a family in the Hundred Acre Wood.